MY LITTLE B

BIG BIBLE PROMISES

BY L. J. SATTGAST

ILLUSTRATIONS BY SUSAN REAGAN

Gold 'n' Honey
BOOKS

MY LITTLE BOOK OF BIG BIBLE PROMISES

published by Gold 'n' Honey Books
a part of the Questar publishing family

©1996 by L. J. Sattgast
Illustrations ©1996 by Susan Reagan
Design by David Uttley (D² DesignWorks)

International Standard Book Number: 1-57673-021-2

Printed in the United States of America

For information:
QUESTAR PUBLISHERS, INC. · POST OFFICE BOX 1720 · SISTERS, OREGON 97759

96   97   98   99   00   01   02   03 — 10   9   8   7   6   5   4   3   2   1

God made a lot of promises.
We find them in the Bible.
God must think they are very important,
because he made a PROMISE about his promises:

The Lord is faithful to all his promises
and loving toward all he has made.

PSALM 145:13

WHAT DO YOU NEED?

Your mom or dad
know what you need.
They give you good morning hugs
and good night kisses
and lots more in between.

They know that you need
good food to eat
and something to drink
and clothes to wear
and a cozy place to sleep.

God knows what you need too.
He said, "I am like a shepherd,
and you are like my little lamb."
So don't worry, little lamb.
God will take care of you,
and your mom and dad too!

The Lord is my shepherd,
I shall not want.

PSALM 23:1

LOTS TO LEARN

There are so many
wonderful things to learn!
How to dress yourself.
How to hold your spoon.
How to brush your teeth.

Your mom or dad or other
people who love you teach you
many of these wonderful things.
And when you forget,
they remind you and help you
to do the right thing.

God has some very special things
he wants to teach you too.
We read about them in the Bible.
I'm so glad God cares enough
about you and me
to teach us good things!

I will instruct you and teach you
in the way you should go.

PSALM 32:8

WHAT IS YOUR NAME?

Do you have a name?
What a silly question!
Of course you do!
You have a first name
and a last name, and
maybe even a middle name!

Your name tells me
who you are and what
family you belong to.
Everyone who loves you
knows your name!

Does God know your name?
What a silly question!
Of course he does!
That's because he loves you
so very much,
and you belong to him!

I have called you by name;
you are mine.

ISAIAH 43:1

NEVER TOO BUSY

Why are grownups so
busy all the time?
Just when you want your mom
to play a game with you
she says, "I have to fix dinner."

And no one ever has the time
to read all the books
you would like them
to read with you.

God understands.
He knows that grownups
sometimes forget what it was like
when they were as young as you.
But God is never too busy.
You can talk with him
anytime you want!

*Let the little children
come to me.*

LUKE 18:16

HOLD MY HAND

When you stand
by a busy street,
you can watch all the cars
go whizzing by.
But how will you get
to the other side?

Then your dad grabs your hand.
"Hold on tight!" he says.
At just the right moment
you and your dad
race across the street
and safely reach the other side.

God knows that there
will be many times
when you will wish that you
could hold someone's hand.
So he made you
a very special promise.

For I am the Lord, your God,
who takes hold of your right hand
and says to you, Do not fear; I will help you.

ISAIAH 41:13

SOMEONE WHO CARES

You can have so much fun
running down the sidewalk
chasing a playful puppy!
But if you trip and fall
and skin your knee,
the fun is over.

36

That's when you hope
that there's someone nearby
who can pick you up
and give you a hug and a kiss
and a Band-aid.

God sees everything that happens.
He knows when you are hurt
or sad or disappointed.
And if you're paying attention,
you'll know that his arms
are wrapped around you too.

The Lord upholds all those
who fall and lifts up all
who are bowed down.

P S A L M   1 4 5 : 1 4

GOD IS WITH YOU

Hurray! This is the day!
You are going on a trip.
It could be someplace exciting.
Maybe you've been there before,
or maybe you're going someplace new.

How will you travel? By car?
By train? By airplane?
Will you take some of your
favorite books and toys?
And who will go with you?
Your father? Your mother?
Your sister or brother?

Don't forget that someone else
will go with you on your trip.
And he will be there
when you reach the end
of your journey.
Can you guess who it is?

I myself will go with you.

EXODUS 33:14

ALWAYS THERE

Wouldn't it be nice
if things lasted longer?
The flowers we picked.
The chocolate ice cream cone.
The visit to the park.

And wouldn't it be nice
if all the people we loved
could be with us all of the time?
You and I know
that isn't the way things are.

But no matter what,
we can be sure of one thing:
That God's love will never end,
and he will always stay with us.
Nothing can keep us away
from God's love!

Never will I leave you;
never will I forsake you.

HEBREWS 13:5

WHAT'S WRONG?

Sometimes, everything turns out
just the way you want it to.
The sun is shining,
your friend comes over to play,
and your mother bakes your favorite
peanut butter cookies.

But sometimes, things don't
turn out the way you want them to.
You have a fight with your friend,
so you have to come inside.
And then it starts to rain!

God knows how you feel.
He's ready to forgive you
when you do something wrong.
And he can even turn bad things
into good things!

And we know that in all things
God works for the good
of those who love him.

ROMANS 8:28

SNUGGLE UP!

Isn't it fun to be near
someone you love?
"Grandma," you might say,
"let's read a book!"
Then the two of you squeeze
into one big chair
with your favorite picture book.

Or you might ask Grandpa
to tell you stories
of when he was your age.
"Sure, Partner!" he says,
and up you go onto his lap.

Yes, it's fun to be near
someone you love.
God must think so too,
because he promised to be
near you all the time—
as close as the air you breathe
and the whisper of wind
on your cheeks.

The Lord is near to all who call on him.

PSALM 145:18

64

SOMEONE IS COMING

When someone special is coming
to your house, what happens?
The house is scrubbed clean, and
the wonderful smell of freshly
baked goodies comes from the kitchen.

You get to help too.
You pick up your books and toys,
take a bath, and put on clean clothes.
Then you wait by the window
hoping to be the first one to see
your very special guest.

The Bible tells us that someone
very special is coming.
It is Jesus, God's only Son.
No one knows just when he will come.
It could be today, or tomorrow,
or many years from now.
But when we see him,
what a happy day that will be!

I will come again.
JOHN 14:3

SAFE AT NIGHT

When the sun goes down
and the shadows come
to cover up the world
like a soft blanket,
then you know that it's time
to say your prayers and go to bed.

Your room looks different at night,
and you can hear sounds that you
couldn't hear during the noisy day.
Tick! Tock!
Swish! Woosh!
Cricket! Cricket!

If night time noises and shadows
make you feel afraid,
remember that God is with you.
He made the noisy day
and the quiet night,
and he has promised to take care
of you and keep you safe.

I go to bed and sleep in peace.
Lord, only you keep me safe.
PSALM 4:8